To Fran

MW01290172

Mystical Poems
by
Three Contemporary
New England Writers

Carol Mays

Richard Bachtold

Nina Andersen

May God continue to
bless and keep you.

Love,
Carol

Library of Congress Control Number:
2011919394

ISBN Number:
978-1466472594

Published in West Brookfield,
Massachusetts

Available at:

www.amazon.com
www.idyllicproductions.org
www.creative-connections.org

"The most beautiful and profound emotion we can experience is the sensation of the mystical."

--Albert Einstein

"From the eyesight proceeds another eyesight and from the hearing proceeds another hearing and from the voice proceeds another voice eternally curious of the harmony of things with man . . . the soul has never once been fooled and never can be fooled . . . every man shall be his own priest."

--Walt Whitman

"People ask me how I make music. I tell them I just step into it. It's like stepping into a river and joining the flow. Every moment in the river has its song. So I stay in the moment and listen."

--Michael Jackson

Table of Contents

Introduction

This inspired book of poems is a unique collection by three contemporary New England poets who write in the long tradition of mysticism—a very ancient tradition that spans various works by Homer, Rumi, Shakespeare, Blake, Wordsworth, Emerson, Whitman, Yeats, Rilke to Ginsberg. Also, this important heritage is a vital part of all faith traditions.

These new poems will offer you a special opportunity to explore, meditate on, and sense a oneness of nature, creation . . . whatever you experience as universal divine energy or God. We trust that you will read these poems as wisdom "messages in a bottle" with a true, open heart, so you may experience in your own way a oneness of all Life.

This seems so necessary in today's troubling times of anxiety, strife, divisions, confusion, uprootedness, and fear. We hope and pray these heart-felt poems, as a gift to you, may in some way draw you closer to your truer home of peace, trust, and connectedness to this invisible, evolving, golden Kingdom of the All.

--Richard Bachtold

Connections to Nature

A Mystical Blade of Grass

As the sacred sun with a thousand
    shining mysteries
rises over the distant mountaintop,
a lone, reflective blade of grass
prays a poem in a dark hidden valley
that reveals in a secret flash of light
the mystical harmony and beauty
that eternally sustains
the still silent voice that daily resurrects
the known and unknown.

                                    -- R.B.

A Woodland Walk

The pensiveness of the sky
is broken by the cry of a crow,
by trees distilling intimacy
and moist, vibrant expectancy.
Violets, ferns, and birches
share life-giving vapors.
The chalk-bleak horizon
and pungent, poignant odors
whisper sonorous secrets.
The visitor is enveloped
in this pithy, soulful world,
all cells saturated
with a suggestive sustenance.

--C.M.

I Belong

I belong to the sunshine,
to the multi-transcendent colors of the
  rainbow.
I belong to the earth,
in the fragrant essence of the flowers' spring,
in the silent growth beneath the seeds of the
  warming earth.
I belong to the animals' creaturehood,
whose birth and death exist seasonally with the
  wonders of my heart.
I belong to the stars,
to the wonders of the world,
to the wonders of the universe.
I belong to love, in its infinite and unspoken
  depths.
I belong to myself, and myself to all that is.

--N.A.

Peace Pagoda Pond Meditation

A saintly Silence calls,
a gentle Silence that embraces voices
of whispering breezes and croakings of frog
  choirs
while all sing with a glowing light from the
  stone bridge,
which becomes a passionate finger pointing
to another Kingdom reflected
in the childlike purity of a surrounding white
  lotus blossoming pond—
all revealing, proclaiming a poetic crossing
  over
to the reigning perpetual Power
  of timeless perfecting Peace.

                                        --R.B.

Innocence

Younger than I am now—
innocent, within ignorance—
the meadows enchanted me,
and the stars
kissed me goodnight.

--N.A.

Faded Glory

The light once so bright
In the humble dandelion,
The power that amazed us
In the migrating birds,
The patterns so intriguing
In frost on the window
Are not lost forever, merely
Held in reserve,
Awaiting sweet release
From the numbing effect
Of fixed preoccupations,
From the stealthy separation
Of projected self-propulsion.

--C.M.

From a Child

Something's wild in the woods tonight—
Something crisp in the breeze.
There's some sweet scent in the shadows.
Hundreds of creatures, hiding out
with eyes and ears wide open.
It seems to me that the forest itself,
young and true, yet ages old,
Is hovering here and everywhere
in a long, black, sparkling cloak.

--C.M.

Circling Silence

As the bright blue dream of deep dawn
sings again with the dew-draped grass
  of waking Earth,
a blazing red sun joyously reaches another
time for the high peak of the distant mountain
and intones a secret song of blessing
with pregnant prophetic words
that die daily
yet live forever in this divine
circling blue dream of Silence
that echoes a distant drumming
in harmony with the heartbeats of a multitude
of mysterious night Hymns.

                                        --R.B.

The Jeweled Grass

The early morning beams of sunlight silently,
    gently caressed
each dew-blade of grass refracting, revealing,
now sparkling red, blue, and yellow jewels
on this mysterious landscape, all an often
    unnoticed sign,
 a gift now to newly awakened eyes
 from the somehow completely illuminated
    Universe
which calls me, once again, to my eternal
    Oneness with the All,
and I step forth into this new day with no fear.

                                        --R.B.

Heavenly Blue Morning Glories

Early morning sparkling sunlight
shined so deeply through the
bright blue morning glories and
revealed a sacred-shimmering
of glowing flowers that, for a moment,
timelessly transformed
all of the surrounding landscape.

--R.B.

Bristles

The graceful boughs of the cypress tree
draped their arches some ninety feet high,
bristling like malachite crystals
into the Persian blue, lucid sky.

As the four o'clock sun illumined the
  needles,
and I gazed toward the sharpening summit,
a distilled purity settled in me,
a condensed refreshment, refinement.

I wished that one of the ones I love
could share this pointed pleasure with me,
could feel this pristine exultation
and know in his heart what I felt.

Faces of dear ones appeared for review,
from the thinnest to the stoutest,
from the shortest to the tallest,
but each had his own distractions.

I sought to keep this treasure secure
and protect it from dissipation,
as I was sure to get lost as well
in matters more common and complex.

I fancied to entrust it to a bird
and by loaning it to this kindred spirit,
thereafter, when glimpsing such a creature,

to feel a whimsical remembrance.

Alas, even the birds were flying by
and the squirrels were packing for winter,
so wistfully I prepared to leave,
resigned to a lonely reverie.

I had but set out on my way
when a gray-haired stranger, passing by,
paused and remarked on the singular
    beauty.
Her words became my souvenir.

                                    --C.M.

Dancing Dragonflies

Before the sinking of the summer sun,
a thousand dragonflies dance
among fleeting rays of sunlight,
weaving all together into a ritual
of unique beauty that for a moment
captures a rare glimpse of eternity.

--R.B.

The Ocean, the Crescent Moon, and the Circle of Creation

In the darkening dance of trembling
    twilight,
when the threshold between Heaven and
    Earth awakes,
 the ever open-eyed white-crested waves
 constantly roar with their prophetic voices
 and break across a dark disappearing
 rock wall as a wild white glow
 of a mystical crescent moon
 is being enfolded by a silent blue
 eternally evolving circle of Creation.

                                        --R.B.

To a Cedar

I had nearly forgotten who I was
Until I sensed your easy strength
  and heard the timelessness
  of your years;
Until I caught the sparkle
  of your lacy light
  and showered
  in your fragrance
Until I recognized your verdancy
  jumping the primal circuit.

--C.M.

Freedom's View

As the wind sighs and trees sound their gentle
  air,
a true reality lies within.
Within a snowflake, a raindrop, a speck of
  sand,
within all passion and desire,
the answers can be found.
The circular, unfinished questions
live amongst the branches within every leaf.
And so we reach inside our minds,
to invisible stars and worlds,
and gaze upon in splendor, through the
  window of illusion,
and see the wings of the wind
open into the mirror of freedom's view.

--N.A.

Ancient Oak-Oracle

Under the skin-bark of the ancient oak,
Tree of Life, lives rings of growth,
around the heartwood, circle-records of
    years,
seasonal changes, transformations –
all a language so deep that it echoes
from the Silence of the Earth.
How many days and how many nights remain
for our faithful tree-oracle?
How many tree-words will speak
of the circling Life and Death story?
And so this courageous tree-spirit
still cries out in these darkest of nights.
And so this prophetic poet
still proclaims out loud and long and
patiently awaits our daily response.
Will we ever hear?
Will we ever hear?
This question is Life.
The answer is our one Life.

                                    --R.B.

To Iris

Cooling, soothing, blue,
Delicate lady
With understated frills,
Sweet, yet bold,
Starkly free,
Growing wild near
Reed and marsh:
In bygone eras,
Perhaps one by your name
Sprang, like Athena,
From the forehead of Zeus,
For sometimes now,
With penetrating purity
And Olympic skill,
You leap at will
Through human eyes
To reclaim your origin
In the temple of the mind,
Encircling the eye
As a rainbow, the sky,
Garnishing our thoughts
With a pristine hope.

--C.M.

Wild River

River Run, River Run,
wild River, song of mystery,
run through our dream.
Wild River Run through our awakening
and lead us Home again,
Home again to the call of the loon,
or speak to us with the soaring of the
   hawk,
or the dance of the full white moon as it
   fades
in the distant night sky.
River Run, faithful wild River Run as we
freely flow
With your primal poem, becoming
one with your eternal journey to the sea,
ocean of the mystical One,
the ever circling Kingdom,
River Run, River Run, wild River Run.

                  --R.B.

June

Wild, ecstatic, frivolous roses,
Haphazardly draping in staccato pink
The grassy embankment.
Bubbling, gleeful, like so many corsages
On fresh-faced girls at a
High school prom.
Cheerful, radiant, intricate charms,
Proffering subliminal messages
Of joy and hope rekindled.

                                   --C.M.

Shades of Green

In shades of green
I lie beside the flowing silver stream
cooling in the forest green deep and dark
with shapely leaves and green vine hearts
soft colored shades of pastel greens
and every shade of plant life in between
I rest my soul
upon the long stemmed grasses low
and dream a dream
of moist soft living shades of green.

--N.A.

Sunday Morning – August, 2009

In the distant morning meadow,
in the center of wind-blown
wild white daisies,
the landscape reveals
the trinity of three wild geese
with just their long necks
and heads visible like periscopes
that seemed to be seeking
and finding their natural
homeland of fulfilled dreams
before the turning towards the night.

--R.B.

Golden Autumn Moments

In golden autumn moments
When leaves fall softly down
Touching earth's moist sacred solemn ground
Are glowing shaded forests of yellow orange
  brown
And smelling scented sandalwood
Perfumes the autumn days
Fields long with unending sand-tipped grasses
  sway
Beneath the slanting shadows
Outstretched below the sunshine's autumn rays
Beyond the fields and sky
All around us fall has captured hearts for miles
  and miles
With memories wide of windy whispering open
  falling skies
Beneath our bodies' happy yellow smiles
Are brightly colored leaves piled high and high
Remembered times of memories sweet and
  tender
Brings life to gone by days of bright September
As woodlands welcome fall's seasoned
  surrender.

--N.A.

October Fest

Homes so recently abandoned
for Sunday swims and picnics
Have become indoor respites
from the restless chill of change.

Secure, still days have vanished
with hazy meadows humming.
Fireflies have met their end,
replaced with jack-o'-lanterns.

Now forewarning breezes,
stealthy, crisp, and vibrant
Pierce preoccupations,
uncovering reckless impulses.

Now uncanny images,
voices of chance and charm,
Bide their ghostly time
to tease mortals hitherto content.

Darts and dashes of circumstance,
figures of flitting moments,
Are creatures mysteriously born,
skipping towards certain death.

So what, if the end is approaching;
the witches' brew is bubbling--
The whispers of all moans and laughs,
the collage of dreams and desires.

Now is the ecstasy of flinging
one's fate to the unrefined choir--
The discordant sounds and initiatives
of many spirits and springs.

Grinning gourds and goblins
bless this annual surprise—
This primal burst of forces
that refuse once more to be quenched.

--C.M.

The Crow Song

Someday, somehow, somewhere
on the forgotten road beside
the forsaken stone wall will
sing one transforming black crow
with an ever deepening song,
a poem only heard
by one awakened outward-
bound poet, a sacred Hymn that
will echo forever from the ever faithful
    Silence.

                              --R.B.

Autumn Red Maple

A red maple, an old faithful friend, has blessed,
   once again,
the harvest time landscape with a royal carpet
   of crimson winged leaves
that have freely fallen to enrich our earthly
   home
and nourish underground seeking roots.
Above ground, the outstretched longing arms
   of the tree,
naked now, reveal brown bones
   as the stately tremendous trunk
stands steadfast throughout our darkening days.
One tree season has ended.
Another cycle with its stark signs of necessary
   sacrifice
has begun patiently to await the turning to Life.

--R.B.

The Forgotten Old Oak

During the transforming mystery of autumn,
on a lonely edge of a long journey,
on a faithful margin of a path
through a secret, forgotten abode
of solitude and Silence
singing with the drama of Heaven and Hell,
where few seek any longer
what few remember as Home,
a solitary old oak with broken branches
blooms one last time with miraculous
multi-colored leaves and creates
a final poem of harmonious vision,
before embracing the sacred circling
silent song of winter to await rebirth.

--R.B.

The Autumn Sunflower

In the mystery of autumnal light,
in the center of the old farmer's
garden of brown corn stalks,
stood one towering, stately
sunflower blessed with its
glowing yellow head gently
embraced with the touch
of morning breezes as all
lovingly spoke to the rising
sun about the turning of
seasonal time before winter's death.

--R.B.

Wild White Rose Poem

As winter approached, a lone wild white rose,
a pure poem that had lived by a forsaken stone
    wall
and glowed in the light of whispering winds,
    died unknown, unheard,
yet one of its small black seeds will faithfully
    gift Life
that will somehow, some way, become a
    necessary part
    of the flowering spring landscape
belonging to, forever singing on, the one
    evolving Poem.

                        --R.B.

The Poet and the Faithful
Fish Brook Hymn at Twilight

In the depths of dark December
while north winds whispered
through broken oak boughs,
the hermit-poet, priest of the banished,
  forsaken, and forgotten,
sought a solitary refuge at twilight
in an eternal holy hymn of faithful Fish
  Brook
as it danced joyfully over ancient rocks
with its secret call for a new Paradise on
  Earth.

--R.B.

The Oak Trees Speak

After the blinding snow,
the light of the morning revealed
that creative winds had sculpted,
on selected shimmering dark oak
    branches,
words of white in an ancient language
for newly opened eyes,
which beheld these transformed trees
as white-robed oracles.

                                        --R.B.

Nature's Friends

The wind comes upon an open sky
with a flowing melody that melts
the glazing icicles hanging in a
starburst of colors—a reflection of the
sun's warming friends.

In the essence of season's time,
one becomes the other; the other
becomes the one. The wind becomes the
sun, as the sun's light blows droplets of
    water and color together,
mixing in a fury of shine and light.

Warming to each other, these two
are old friends recapturing the
moods and motions within each.

One cannot be without the other.
They are intimately connected—the sun, the
water, the wind. No season lives without its
    motions,
no motion without its untimely moods,
blending, shifting and constantly merging,
shapefully becoming part of all.
Nothing is left untouched, nothing is left
    unknown--
Partners in an eternal, beautiful splendor of
    form and color.

                                    --N.A.

The Return of Red-Winged Blackbirds

Toward the end of the long winter, the
    morning unfolds
with the gifting of the landscape with a new
    sun-filled day.
This glistening spring day reveals the annual
    arrival of red-winged blackbirds
as they embrace the dormant apple tree,
    dressing the nude branches,
proclaiming that winter wood will not be dead
    forever,
despite the loss of vital sap, green leaves, or
    red fruit.
In the midst of these revealing spring signs,
    a seasonal wisdom is born:
Even in a time of apparent loss and death
one may still see potential, possibility, and
    promise.
This lone old apple tree lives now, reborn,
 prophesying with its singing red-winged
    blackbirds,
 circling with omens from another world
 about an approaching spring,
 another new season of abundant Life.

--R.B.

Little Oak Tree

Little oak tree, hidden in the
deep dead brown grass by the
side of the abandoned road
speak to me again of Life.
Let me hear your singular passionate
  voice
embraced by the dancing wind.
Tell me again of your necessary
unforgotten ancient secrets.
Talk to me of your green-dream
of seed-birth, silent growth struggle,
and faithful forever Hope
rooted in future acorn seedlings,
all remembered wisdom gifting
the new evolving landscape.

                                    --R.B.

Only Words

Only words, only words, only words
I have to give to you, our world.
O, will they be enough?
I give you, our world, words
from our sunlight as it shines
each day across our waking landscape.
I give you words from our moon
as it graces dreams of each night
with gentle moonbeams.
How I weep for more than
these humble poetic signs of Life,
symbols that always long to somehow
embrace the unseen choir of angels
that ever praise.
O, how will I, this poet, continue
to hear, even today
with the deepening silence, more words
from the raven dancing across the black sky,
or the song of singing stream
flowing over rocks,
or the fleeting wind rustling through the
  trees?
Yet, always, somehow, somewhere in
this tremulous trembling seeking and finding
lives the unforgotten wisdom where
Poet, Earth, and Word become One and this
  gift
 journeys on to another Home.

                              --R.B.

46

Identities and
Relationships

In the Beginning . . .

A light has always been glowing
close to the heart of the universe.
Over the course of time and evolution,
we as mortals have lived in fragile
  transience.
Yet flickering in the soul
is the sublime, primordial sparkle.
In this ember born of the primal fire,
the transient contains the immortal
and the infinite caresses the finite.
Through the morass of earthly chaos,
the crystal beacon shines, and
its power has not been extinguished.

--C.M.

An Ember of Being

Light are the particles
Surrounding my being
Free, crystallized energy
Flowing and streaking
Through glowing sunrays
Transparent multi falling raindrops
Vitalized as midnight thunder
Echoing to the skies.

--N.A.

Direction

With every desire
of whole selfhood
Is the loving direction
of true freedom.

--N.A.

In Youthful Splendor

In my youth, when in my splendor,
when my body's soul was beauty slender,
I knew the person I was meant to be
was in my Self's authenticity.
My heart of gold was open wide.
The world saw through my joyful smile.
engaged in nature's beauty, youth
My tongue spoke words of heartfelt truth.
hopeful of all I was to be—
A freeing soul; a soul of me—
I felt the pulse of earthly gods,
of greener trees amidst the fogs,
Meandering their branches tall,
beneath soft grasses, yellow flowers small,
The meadows' sunken velvet green,
with spreading incense sweet perfume
that beckoned lovers to nature's dream,
Till purple nights fell into star-white
    moonbeams.
and even in the moment's time
that lasted longer in our passionate minds,
We knew we came to change the world
for love and peace and joy sublime,
To help each other's soul to shine,
a single tear of human fear,
which love could soften close and near,
To lead us out of fearful nights
upheld in us by golden lights
To feel in love's compassions right.

We know of Spirit's coming way
that hope and love frees all someday,
An inner faith, an inner word,
spoken within us, from Godly worlds,
That we may grasp in age, as in our youth,
the sages wisdom spoken truth.

--N.A.

On Becoming My Poet

I live and die the eternal call to poetic Life.
I add my voice to the faithful
flowering river of priestly Song.
I put a shoulder to the plow
for the light of poetic peace.
I silently seek the
word that lives in both the
light of day and the dark of night.
I faithfully seek the Poetry
in all wisdom traditions.
I daily awake and open
the inner eye to become one
with its poems of our Earth,
every rock, tree, animal, and human.
I constantly chant my prayer –
poems to the fleeting winds of time.
I am the old wise one, but
forever the circling young poet.
I finally gift my poems of
Life to you, all my sons
and daughters of our Earth,
to carry on in my memory
to another Kingdom.

--R.B.

I Listen

Once upon a time
I saw the light
of my own words and heart.
Now I listen to
the heart of the universe
And feel its vast motion
inside my soul.

--N.A.

Bifocals

Through the window of connectedness,
the landscape grins.
Introspective roadways?—
nursery clay.
All the somber mountains—
props in a play.

--C.M.

I Am

I am a purple violet

A soft shade of color that speaks wonders to the
earth.

I am a shimmering wave that sprays a foam of
white onto the sand.

I am the old woman's past, her memories of
gold,

Her heartache, the furrowed brow, the years of
age that are written upon her now.

I am passion, touching feelings, aching in truth.

I am a child, a question, innocent and wild.

I am the sorrow I see and all the tears that
engulf my being.

I am a rainbow, light, multi-colored,
transcendent.

I am the love that I give.

I am all that I am.

I encompass all that I experience.

--N.A.

The Comforter

Bristling yet beguiling winds are
driving snow sheets through the dark,
and, secured by brick and lamp,
I draw a comforter to my breast,
one woven by humanity.

I sense that each quickening gust
is pulling through the loom of time
life's many multi-colored threads.

A hickory brown is borne to me
of ships defying depths and dangers,
carrying dreams and heartaches.

Glistening now—the lucent blue
of fertile, percolating minds,
genome maps and software.

I feel the orange of affection,
hearth and smiles and homecomings,
the warmth of song and story.

The blinking silver of fantasy,
visionaries, piercing sterility--
castles, stars, utopias.

Here is a filament of frothy pink
comedies, dances, and levity,
play and spontaneity.

The looming strands of swarthy black
necessities, death, and armies,
relentless in their marching.

The golden promise of sacred texts,
altars, candles, hope,
encoded and translated.

Emerging, the green of recent growth,
rites of spring and passage,
learning and inner progress.

With such a large and lustrous blanket
in which to sink, like a new-born babe,
I'll toss some folds to you, as they will
easily stretch from here to there.

--C.M.

I Am

I am the road not often traveled.
I am the singing river
that flows endlessly to the distant sea.
I am the question and the answer.
I am the last oak leaf freely falling
to the waiting earth home.
I am the homeless, the outcast,
the oppressed, the feared,
the outsider, and the enemy.
I am the singer and the song.
I am the only apple on the old tree
in the abandoned orchard.
I am the lost poem always
waiting for the eternal reader.
I am the unseen daisy dying
beside the forsaken rock wall.
I am the saint and the sinner.
I am the faithful goose flying homeward.
I am the word and the silence.
I am the lone wolf howling
nightly to the fading moonlight.
I am the single spear of bent
grass ever seeking the touch
of the rising sun.
I am the forgotten, rejected poet.
I am the known, the unknown,
the heard, the unheard,
the seen, the unseen,

the Earth, the Heaven,
the soul, the spirit,
the death and the life.
I am the muse, the madman,
the mystic, and the prophet.
I am the journey, the home,
the beginning, the end,
the creator and the creation.
I am the vision, the transformation,
the imagination, and the possibilities.
I am the history, all sacred
traditions, the new, the old,
the finite, and the everlasting
I am all this and more.
I am the All! I am!

--R.B.

The Shadowed Smile

Behind your faces of disguise,
You hide your life within your eyes.
Somehow I felt
I could reach inside tomorrow
to quiet all
your longing sorrows,
Where others had failed
and you had denied
Your dreams to die,
and winds to wash your tears aside
While loneliness surrounds a shadowing
smile.

--N.A.

Broken Horses

We long for relationships
that know no borders,
In which hearts can roam free,
frolicking with each other,
and galloping at will
through fields and streams
in broad daylight,
and spontaneous affections
can nuzzle unrestrained.

Yet on our humble ranch,
it is the broken horses
that we so often ride.
Connections become curtailed
that once headed for the horizon,
by trial and error taught
to shield certain wounds
and mind necessary fences,
in many a peculiar pasture.

--C.M.

Crossways

Summer night pulsing
Streak of jets landing
Sapphire lights winking

Minds ricocheting
Lovers embracing
Cologne, silk caressing

Muscle maneuvering
Luggage uplifting
Strength celebrating

Interstate soaring
Windows, dash, dancing
Jazz and soul rocking

Frequency sampling
Circuits infusing
Earth-force vibrating.

--C.M.

Your Eyes

No finer jewels exist on earth
than your sparkling eyes to me.
Like mirrors set in an infinite row,
displaying your hopes, thoughts,
    fears, and joys,
They reveal all hopes, thoughts,
    fears, and joys,
Reflecting lights and skies and oceans,
Portals to space, time, and humanity—
to all that really matters.

                                --C.M.

The Silence of Love

Lost in the eyes of love,
with words that have no meaning,
The words of the wordless,
unspoken, without sound,
Beneath the reality of touch,
yearning for its loving rebirth.

--N.A.

Nathan and Sarah

Two hearts were called,
Amidst the cacophony of life,
Amidst the fruitfulness of life.
Evolving from timelessness,
Moving in the center of existence.

Now each finds in the calling,
Beyond the restrictions of space,
An ever more central reality,
An ever more expanding reality,
Sensing even through dissonance,
Home, in its ever-pulsing joy.

--C.M.

Forever in My Heart

You are an ocean of movement in my soul,
a wave upon the gentle sands of my heart.
You are forever an eternal part
of the intimate being within me.
You travel like the winds of time
through the seasons of my mind.
You encircle the light
that gives my eyes their sight.
You are the leaf that grows green and free,
filling its reach of sky into me.
You are the face whose grace and form
have lived unlettered and unworded in love
    unborn.
You are the soul whose growing essence,
grows beneath the silence of my unending
    heart.
You are the glass of the window of my
untouched dreams. You wander into the
world of many faces, yet speak no words
that others hear. Your voice leaves its
silent sound under the skin of my life.
You fill every space, every moment,
with the gaze of your face.
You enter into the time of my mind
where nothing begins or ends, or says hello
or good-bye. The blaze of your tone,
the song of your being unfolds into lights.
and sends its beauty outreaching the stars
of love within my soul,

And my soul, it sings
to rejoice in one union in its love.
You are the soul
whose glowing essence
merges untimely one into the other,
Forever in my heart.

                              --N.A.

Time
and
Eternity

A Moment's Reflection

A moment's birth into existence, is a moment's
    imprint into eternity
upon the invisible airy winds of time.
A moment's reflection never gone or lost,
Absorbed into the timeless universe.
Sucked into unending timeless tunnels of
    swirling light,
Speeding across our infinite minds,
Rebirthing into our nightly dreams.
A moment of reflection, an endless now of
    nows.

                                        --N.A.

October 15, 1991

Scattered images flicker,
   as an evening passes:
Leaves riding the rain,
   in a bittersweet farewell;
A singer's warmth beamed
   to thousands of vehicles;
Ghosts swinging from strings
   in a Halloween display;
Sakharov's casket carried
   in a documentary;
A boy brimming with youth,
   delivering news on
A Union birthing nations,
   eight thousand miles away.

To work-weary eyes,
   strained and myopic,
Just routine impressions
   of another hectic day.
But these are the pulses
   of the unfolding cosmos,
The eddies and streams of
   forces and formations.
Being a mere ripple
   in this dazzling array
Is to be soaked to the core
   with a quintessential gift.

--C.M.

The Banquet

Who is God,
but the connecting link,
the evolution of energy.
And love, likewise,
the dissolution of separation,
the current between gaps,
the transfusion of forces,
creativity unbounded.

Out for a stroll,
I am caught up in
three heavenly visions:
a white cloud passing,
a maple fluttering,
and a hornet exploring.
And these divine voices:
the chirping of a finch,
hammering in a yard,
the sound of someone's stereo.

In one common moment,
I am a communicant
in this feast of life--
its continuing burst
of expressions and ambitions,
its multifaceted forms.

Even the dancing Shiva

does not have the arms
to hold so much dear.

"Brother Sun; Sister Moon,"
This is joy undiluted--
We are each related
right to the core
down to the electrons
whizzing in us all.

                                    --C.M.

To Mozart

Upon hearing what you heard
And relayed with such devotion,
The soul arises as a bird from a puddle,
Shaking off its present absorptions,
Abandoning its own reflection,
Drawn toward an infinite horizon,
It's nudged along by wind-borne petals,
Entranced by a piercing blue
In a sheer, receptive sky.

--C.M.

Passwords

There is a hall of plans and schemes,
of efficiency quotas and waiting chores,
errands, reminders, and deadlines.
Here myriad estimates of productivity
appear, and nag, and vanish.

A stone-faced guard attends the door.
He's fit and trim and serious.
His feet appear to be soundly placed;
his posture well-assumed.

There is a garden of sun and streams,
of beckoning paths and flickering lights,
of roses and crystal skies.
Here myriad tones of the musical muse
appear, and wave, and vanish.

A carefree guardian leans on the gate.
She's lithe and soft and sweet.
She wears a robe of green and blue,
a flowing belt of crimson.

The sense of time is what determines
 one's location at any moment.
The map can be found in the mind.
 One scuttles into the hall, beset,
 but meanders into the garden.

The password to the hall is this:
"Time is of the essence."
One quickly salutes the impatient guard
and strides towards one's intentions.

The garden, though, may seem a mirage—
the gate an apparition,
unless one responds to the guardian's kiss
and sighs, "Time is eternal."

                                    --C.M.

Darkness

O, darkness, silver sanctuary of deep Silence,
home of the never-ending cry from the abyss
   of not knowing;
O, darkness, site of the sacred seed
underground,
womb of the Earth, waiting to give birth
to new innocent blue flowers of song;
O, darkness, abode of promising poems,
breath in strong shadows giving Life;
O, darkness, sacred One, heal us,
once again, with the open graciousness and
paradoxical harmony of your mute unknown
   Song.

                              --R.B.

Meditation

In the eye of many whirlwinds
Stays a deep, dark pool,
Tranquil and translucent,
At the vortex of Being,
Forever fed by subtle springs
Which give mysterious birth to
Thoughts pure and lucid
In their easy distillation.
Time is sure to transport, but
Mortality's ride is muffled
In this sweet, serene suspension.

--C.M.

The Eternal Sacrament

This visionary poem is a gift from the Creator,
a secret song rising from sacred Silence,
a celebration of holy communion
offered to all Creation,
so that when death calls,
all life embracing this eternal,
universal sacrament will live.

--R.B.

The Long View

There was a maze of brambles
on my hike toward the summit—
a misprinted map, and
false and tedious paths.
With tenuous steps constrained by vines,
and boots scratched by burrs,
at last I reached the observatory,
still sorely seeking answers
to a deep, persistent quest.
Peering through the telescope,
I saw a flash of unveiled truth,
brilliant as the noon-day sun,
blazing in the darkening sky:
"The life that so confuses you
is given as a two-fold gift:
for eighty years, you have the chance
to glimpse Infinity unfold
and in this precious blip of time,
participate with heart and mind,
in the great, grand evolution."

--C.M.

Unfinished Answers

Searching for unfinished answers
without order or logic.
A beginning without an entrance,
an ending without exits.
Timeless truths and absurdities of the heart,
struggling towards its death and rebirth,
without memory of its speeches and unspoken
  words.
Beneath the all of everything,
lies the meaning in an ordinary blade of grass.

--N.A.

Our One Transformation

In the beginning, is Life about transformation?
Just as the tiny water beetle turns
into a beautiful, blue-tailed dragonfly
or the small green larvae turns
into the royal free-flying monarch,
or the hidden brown acorn seed into
the mighty stately oak, what is our
   earthy journey,
or how do we, or how should we daily change,
evolve and come step by step to the top
of our holy mountain Home?
Some change slowly, some stay the same,
or some somehow daily grow deeper into
their soul-filled true homecoming.
Our new world seeks, awaits,
needs our one compassionate sign.
Our world community seeks, awaits,
needs our one poem of peace,
our one circling note in its all-connected
song of Life, and our journey to the
waiting, needing arms of the All.
And in the end, this new Earth and Heaven
welcomes our one glorious, beyond words,
   transformation.
                                        --R.B.

Encapsulation

Said the water in the can
that was tossed into the Bay,
"Will I continue to exist
 if my can rusts away?"

--C.M.

Consciousness Rhythms

Age is the second coming of the soul's
   celebration to physical life.
Reawakened by the inner wisdom
   of the soul,
A second adolescence of the soul's life,
   meaning and purpose.
Soul rhythms are like waves upon the water's
   shore, flickering in the sunlight
Beaming with life beneath the depths of
   dimensional rhythms.
Age is not an end to the earthly, aging soul;
 It is instead just the beginning to a new
   journey ahead.
 You are coming into a new life,
 So be glad and rejoice--
 Rejoice in the eternity of the soul.
 For all souls travel in living eternity,
 Blessed and loved always by the God of the
   universes.
Look forward to age with peace and safety
  in your hearts,
Knowing that you are an eternal soul of God.
There is no end or beginning,
Just joyful consciousness rhythms of eternity.
Wake up to the truths of your soul.
There is no death as you think of it.
There is no death;
There is only change of form--

There is only life.

Waste no more time on saddened dreams.

Wake up and be alive;

Be joyful in life's moments of eternity.

--N.A.

Amphibians

When life is losing its meaning,
And the glorious colors grow pale,
And death seems the one destination,
Remember the humble toad,
Doomed to spend drier days
Digging deep in the arid ground,
Seeking survival and shelter,
But to be loving and birthing,
It later returns to the flow
Of a resilient milieu that bestows
The clarity of radiant expanse
And the nudges of buoyant kin.

Perhaps the insular, dreary days
Are partly an illusion
And existence points not to the grave,
But to a metamorphosis,
In which we shed these calloused feet
And bathe in the nurturing nexus
Of our birth-home, the sea.

--C.M.

Eternal Wheel of Life

The vision in the nighttime dream
guides our path of Life Home.
Also, every morning awake to the
luminous day, before circling nightly
to other Homeward, threshold signs of Life,
like a singing lace of light from
the radiant sun, or the graceful
deer dancing across the still morning
meadow, or the music of a red leaf
swaying with a gentle wind.
Then, like a wild mad poet,
become one with the signs of
Life and become a necessary word
in the one lyrical song of our
night and day Homeland and
then the eternal Wheel of Life
will turn, once again, with
your precious gift to our one
family of all continuing Creation.

--R.B.

How Many Days to Sing?

How many days?
How many days remain to sing
the one Song?
How many days will the poet be
able to transform life into words that
speak and live the language of the heart,
that sing of the bluebird in flight,
or the faithful sun rising over
the distant mountaintops,
or the gentle breezes caressing the old
oak leaves, or name again the sorrow and
joys of our human family?
This poet rises, one more time
to another day to see the world anew,
to hear the Silence,
to sing into being another world,
and finally calls out with a desperate
plea for all future true poets
with their own faithful new song,
to sing into being again the one evolving
Kingdom.

                                    --R.B.

Landlocked

I tried to describe the ocean
to one who lived well inland
and never had been to the coast
or swam in the cresting waves.
"It seems so infinite," I said—
"both humbling and exalting."
She hastily informed me that
she'd bought a new bikini for
reclining at the local pool.
Then she flicked her cigarette
on half an abalone shell
that once had shimmered in the surf,
until its dislocation.

--C.M.

Dying Sunflower Prayers

In the mystery of autumn twilight,
at the edge of a frost-smitten garden,
stood three dying sunflowers
with their brown seed-laden heads
bowed in their final prayers,
and their falling seeds
like poems left by dying poets
seek a new earthbound, but Heavenly Home
where their miraculously sown seeds
will resurrect through new golden generations.

--R.B.

The Poet's Gift

These are my words to my beloved world,
 the Poem of summation of many lived
 previous precious heart-intuitions.
This Poem is born in a distant dream
 in the dark night and lives
 in the rising sun of every new day.
This Poem is the small seed sown
 In the womb of all evolving Life.
This Poem is your journey from seed
 to ripening song, a single struggling song
 that sings of faithful growth with every
 new song of the Tree of Life.
 a song of our Earth's truth that is proclaimed
 by each rock, tree, and animal, a wisdom-
   song harvest
 gleaned from a silent garden of secret,
 selected, true words,
 a strong song of solid rock inherited as a gift
 from all the faithful poetic ancestors.
This Song-Poem remains in your
 prophetic dream in the darkest of nights.
This Song-Poem remains in every poetic-seed
   of compassion
you sow whenever, wherever they are
   planted in the garden of Life.
This Song-Poem remains in your faithful journey
 even when the words of death descend.

94

This Song-Poem is you.
This Song-Poem is always about resurrection.
This Song-Poem is eternal.

--R.B.

Beacons

The eyes of heavenly beacons
Peek out from amidst the shadows,
Like so many playful stars
Behind a mist-blown sky—
Or the diffuse glow of street lamps
Draped with sculpted snow.
From songbirds to sonatas,
From meteors to mantras,
They veil themselves in fetching garb
And wink at us as a lover.

--C.M.

Visions, Dreams, and Fantasies

Illusions

Illusions without depth
Shape or form
Shadowless infinity
Purpose and meaning
Lying within our
Timeless minds.

--N.A.

A Poem for Your Dream

What is your dream? What daily dream
of yours lives in the darkest night?
How does your one dream die?
Your dream is a fragile,
flickering poem of light, or a gentle
hope of a new world that brightly burns
in an open heart,
or a beacon of truthful compassion in the
darkening days.
Sometimes, too often, in our fearful
trembling world just one word of no may crush
your dream,
or sometimes in our days of antilife unseen
   deadly forces can
block the path of your dream, or sometimes
just the curse of apathy may have
you question your dream.
Only the persistent, strong, courageous
dreamer's dream carries on, only the ever-
 faithful
poet-dreamer of the great prophetic tradition
survives, only the necessary sacrificial one
   willing
to die in and for your dream lives on forever.
Live your dream of beauty, peace, justice, and
   truth.
Live your dream to the end of your days.
Live your dream because no one can ever do
   it for you.

                                    --R.B.

Beyond

Beyond the winds of time,
Beyond the fields of orange fire sunsets,
Beyond the velvet green forest carpets,
Are places within our dreams,
Of purple hazing brilliant light beams,
and lightly floating flying dreams,
With fields of white laced daisies dancing
 and golden illuminated figured spheres prancing
 Beyond us, yet so close near hand--
 A loving place more beautiful than summer land,
Of sweetly smelling rose and violet
and perfumed shades of color lilac.
All is one there, love and joy
that no human heart can give away.
No tears of joy, no moment's pleasure,
can compare to this place of heaven's violet
   heather.
As we dream the dream of dreams,
We enter worlds of spirit-shaded seams
and walk into spirit bodies' bright pure light.
In our hearts and in our minds
I can't forget this experienced time.
And so I take the memory back
to share the love, to prevent the lack
To bring love light wisdom
to all who will listen.
Hear and feel these words I say,
This place is real!
And in our future we will all be there someday.

                                        --N.A.

The Wild Man

In the midnight hour,
he arises and silently walks out
of the deep and dark forest
into our mountaintop dreams and
calls us to remember:
This hairy one dressed in green
tree boughs knows our name.
This Wild Man of the Earth that
sings the Poetry of the King
which proclaims "The One who believes."
This holy One speaks with and for the
towering oak, the howling wolf,
and the grain of sand.
This grief man is nailed to the
cross and wails for the death of
all the innocent wild ones.
This coyote trickster leaves many
tracks, one foot in ice, one in fire to
expose the hunter's dark lies.
This shaman warrior lives and dies his one
  Poem.
Here now on our earthly trembling
trek between light and dark
hear, see, follow again our royal
Wild Man before our final calling
to another Kingdom.

                 --R.B.

An Archetype

Somewhere in an old-growth forest,
a woman smoothly moves amidst
shadows of the pines and hardwoods.
Her mossy gown is verdant green,
her hair twinkles with mica, and
her soul, deep as a midnight sky,
with remote star clusters beaming.
She tends the ruins of an ancient inn
and a bed of ferns and roses.
Many a nomad, passing through,
is revived by her grace and goodness.
Though we can't lay hands on her,
she wanders free within our grasp,
For the ancient inn beguiles us still
in the labyrinths of our minds.

--C.M.

White Words of Life

In the blackest of nights,
the poet fell into a deep sleep
beneath the feet of old oak,
guardian of the sacred grove.
Some time later, this dreamer
awoke remembering the vision
of the night where royal oak
split open to reveal,
for a fleeting moment, a step
into another world, where a golden
haired nymph was prophesying
in her luminous presence
white words of Light about
an astral spirit which has, is,
and forever will call all to belong
to Life in the dark of Death.

--R.B.

Moon Goddess of Poetry

Why do you not see her? Why?
Have you been asleep too long?
Awake! Awake!
Here now see, once again,
the moon mother of sun and ocean waves.
Her celestial chariot drawn by
a gentle team of white deer
is approaching.
She wears a luminous cloak
of dark blue, speckled with stars
and hemmed with the morning dew.
Her head is crowned with
a bouquet of green pine boughs.
Her silent Poem is always
welcomed to our earthly home
by our prayers of stone circles.
She is the everlasting light of
poetic wisdom in the still
night sky awaiting to guide,
illuminate our every uncertain
step on our journey Home.
Here now on our earthly trek
awake, see, serve, follow the
Light of Life, our muse, our moon
goddess of Poetry before the curtain
of Death descends forever.

                      --R.B.

Ghostly Visions

Haunting wanton dreams
knock upon the night.
Ghostly visions caress
the misting air.
Fathoms of loneliness,
weep among their dead.
Silently, souls awaken
whispering in the breeze.

--N.A.

Futility

Out into the rainy streets,
the desolate, deserted byways,
far beyond any visible horizons,
he entrusted his life force--
Energy that came back to him
as so many drafts and drizzles,
accumulating over the years
as puddles that caught his feet
and pounded at his foundations.
He was asked about the saying
that what goes around, comes around;
but the query became an echo,
and his response, too hollow to grasp.

--C.M.

The Siesta

The sky was yellow, with sparkling beams
in iridescent gold
reflected on the pointed hat
of an elf, two centuries old.

The hostess of the hour was sweet
in a robe of mismatched dyes.
She entertained with merely this--
a kiss in her root beer eyes.

The placemats were of baby fern,
woven in intricate green,
and laughter was heard
like the tinkling of bells
near the banks of an ebony stream.

I boarded a raft for an underground cave,
which was carved in a spiral pattern.
The subterranean symphony hall
was draped in coral satin.

At the end of the course, was a water-slide
in hues of ultraviolet,
with children bouncing up and down.
They prevailed upon me to try it.

Though some might want to interpret this,
myself, I'm in no hurry

to analyze such a sweet retreat
which woke me without a worry.

--C.M.

Fantasies

Somewhere,
Music is eternal and dance is the soul
    unleashed.
Emanating from bird nests,
Melodies rise with the sun and stars.
Cellos call from sand dunes and seas.

Somewhere,
Sparkling-haired children in yellow silk,
Sprinkled with sun rays,
Dance with no audience on a hill
Amidst the scent of lilacs, earth, and sun.

Somewhere,
Blue, green, and purple mist mingle at
    evening,
When roses grow without thorns,
And women in glowing robes walk near
    streams
Of snow landing as natural lace.

--C.M.

The Dream

Somewhere on the edge of this world
there dwells no violence, fear, war, and death.
Somewhere on the edge of this world
lives a beautiful country of prophetic poetry
with a great river of healing, flowing
   with compassion for all.
In this sacred land,
all ancient trees sing out with one voice
for the flowering reign of holy harmony.
In this sacred land, all solid rocks cry out from
   the heart
of the darkest nights for days of justice,
and each ensuing dawn proclaims, "All is One,
   and One is All."
Somewhere on the edge of this world
lives the Dream with the perfect Poem,
the Peaceable Kingdom, the everlasting Hope
   and Joy,
And the Home of Eternal Eden.

                        --R.B.

People Awake

Awake! Awake!
Who now remembers sacred seeds sowed
　　by the ancient ones?
Who now hears the drumming?
Who now hears the dancing light in the dark?
The moon now faithfully rises over the
　　distant mountain
weeping for her lost children.
Yesterday, the people gathered around a
　　flaming fire
and became one with the praising moonlight.
Today, the moon's poetry is lost, unknown to
　　dead ears
and a slightless people blinded by the false
　　light of unending "progress."
Awake! Awake!
For our future, let a race of a new people
　　arise,
innocent children uniting, remembering,
　　renaming
ancient secret stories, singing new songs
　　to our faithful moon—
poems celebrating the creative Oneness with
　　our Home
 and forever renewing and healing our
 evolving Universe.

　　　　　　　　　　　　　--R.B.

Progressive Rock

On the energy waves of the eons,
Of lyric and line ever-forming,
One is injected, transported,
With all vibrations bursting
Through the human heart and mind,
The jolting edge of innovation
And every positive passion.

Even the cynic or child may sense,
When riding such a current,
The power native to humanity.
Synapses now malfunctioning
Cannot forever thwart their charge.
Mankind has the voltage needed
To mobilize all the connectors.

--C.M.

113

Heaven

Sing me a song of a
child's laughing eyes.
Teach me the world
from a child's trusting smile.
Show me the gentleness
of a warm summer breeze.
Run me through winds,
grasses and trees.
Find me a place
where there's springtime and honey,
Skies that are blue,
Loves that are true.
Catch me the light
that flows from the stars.
Keep it and seal it
in sugar-made jars.
Sing me a love song,
quiet and nice.
Love me forever
for the rest of my life.

--N.A.

Believe

Catch a star, if it is what you believe.
Let it be your dream.
Grow it wild, fresh and green.
Smell its sweet perfume.
Glimmer in its light.
Shine it golden bright.
For if a man has not his dreams,
He knows not who he is.

--N.A.

Wild Ones

Sophisticated ladies,
embellished by eons,
illusive, enchanting,
with black velvet "eyes,"
and fringed yellow cloaks,
sparkling with diamonds
at midnight and dawn,
Oh, fly me away from
my grey-flooded days,
from the four-lane race
and the file draw maze.
Fly me away from
the chain of the clock
and the sink of necessities.
Bring me in spirit
to magical rendezvous,
to dance by the glint
of the moon on the marsh,
hiding from fireflies,
nudging antennas.

                         --C.M.

Other Worlds

Dancing blue-white beams of a crescent
    moon,
gently slip intermittently through blackened
    clouds,
softly caressing an abandoned red barn,
revealing all as a newly awakened poem,
beckoning for a thousand Other Worlds
to which we long to belong.

--R.B.

The Ecstasy of Thought

Walking wondrously through a soft carpet
  forest,
Leaves crunch beneath my feet,
An only interruption, breaking nature's silent
  stillness
Soft natural echoes encircling shadowing
  pastels
Golden browns, olive greens, sweet incense
  pine
Peering above me as through holes of a
  ceiling
Are patches of blue
The glaring sun's transparent rays
Of yellow pierce my eyes
 I walk on aimlessly, deeply,
Trying to lose myself
To be caught in another dimension of time
 Where existence reality has yet to come
 In my mind, I am caught
 In ecstasy of thought
 That life is but a repeating dream
 Repeating, reliving, creating forever.

--N.A.

Biographical Information

The authors can be reached at:

Candlelight Readers' Circle
P.O. Box 334
West Brookfield
Massachusetts 01585

Carol Mays

Carol Mays has resided in seven states and sought truth through many religious and philosophical traditions. Throughout her life, she has been strongly drawn toward beauty in all its forms.

Carol has been writing poetry for 45 years. Many of the poems in the present volume have been reprinted from previously published books entitled, *Strategies, Poems, & Stories for Holistic Living* and *Images for Wholeness.* Carol has also written a short novel in the magical realism genre entitled, *The Magic-Makers' Carnival.*

Carol currently lives in West Brookfield, Massachusetts and works as a quality assurance coordinator for a foster care agency in Worcester.

Richard Bachtold

Richard Bachtold has passionately followed his calling to poetry for over thirty years. He lives a simple lifestyle on a beloved two-acre homestead in rural Hardwick, Massachusetts. For the most part, inspiration for his creative work comes from the beautiful natural landscape which surrounds him.

For many years, he has independently studied the poetical process, the poetical heritage, and he has dedicated himself to seeking how the aestheticism of poetics is connected to a creative way of living with moral integrity. He has self-published three books of poetry, and his mystical poems with their universal nature have been published in various alternative publications, including *Pilgrimage, Gaian Voices,* and *Original Blessing*.

Nina Andersen

Nina Andersen is a poet who's search for truth
and God has led her into realms of spiritual
experiences, leading to spiritual knowledge and
soul enlightenment. The visions and intensity of
her experiences are expressed through her
poems, in her desire and hope to bring spirituality
and enlightenment to others. She wishes to
remind humankind of its eternal soul, of the love
and joy that is within the universe, and that God is
real and exists everywhere, eternally.

Nina Andersen lives in Hardwick, Massachusetts,
in a yellow-windowed house, surrounded by
nature, flowers, and woodland. She is a poet,
mystic, therapist, and teacher. She presently
teaches Critical Thinking and Problem Solving at
Quinsigamond Community College in Worcester,
Massachusetts.

Postscript

Poetic mysticism has sadly been marginalized in today's world, even within the arena of poetry. However, I feel it is a vital counterweight to countless other endeavors which, if left unchecked, would destroy the human race by pitting person against person, group against group, nation against nation, and humanity against nature.

That is why, without any reasonable expectation of remuneration, I have solicited such poems from two of my most talented friends and woven them together with my own, to form this book. Because they share my vision, Richard Bachtold and Nina Andersen have freely given of themselves, as well.

We hope that the reader has found these words as uplifting and precious as we have.

When my friends shared their poems with me, I felt as though I had been given a treasure chest of diamonds and entrusted with the task of fashioning them into a necklace. They laugh when I tell them this—"maybe diamonds in the rough," they say. But when I compare these poems with others I have read in this genre, I am honored beyond measure.

--Carol Mays

Title Index

Made in the USA
Charleston, SC
05 June 2012